PURE

NAIMA YETUNDE INCE

ABOUT THE AUTHOR

Naima Yetunde Ince is an emerging author of poetry. This is Naima's fifth book.

Naima recognized her purpose and gifts at the tender age of six. She began writing poems that evolved into songs, short stories, stage plays, and more. As she grew older and her faith in God deepened, her purpose became more clear. In doing so, Naima allowed God to use her as a vessel to communicate to others as she dropped gems for more than just herself. Naima has the ability to convey thoughts and ideas—which may be challenging for others to express—that can only be heard and received by words she has written.

Naima says, "I can feel when God is speaking through me and provides the creative license through whatever medium I am working on, be it a spoken word poem or stage play." It's a very special gift to have and Naima does not take it lightly. In fact, she encourages her son to be fortified in his spirit, in his relationship with God; and to know that his purpose is larger than him and his own legacy—depending on the gifts that God gives to him. Naima is a graduate from SUNY Purchase College with a B.A. in Theater Studies. She is a graduate from Pratt Institute with a Master of Professional Studies in Arts and Cultural Management. She has developed her own company entitled N.Y.I Productions LLC where she publishes her own literature and focuses on the full productions of Theater and Film derived from her own work. N.Y.I Productions LLC is Naima Yetunde Ince Productions LLC.

Dedication

For all the women who are survivors
For all the men who uphold the women
For my son who's dreams are worth fighting for

CONTENTS

Introduction	ix
Acknowledgments	xiii
1. In A Heartbeat	1
2. Blue Black Purple	12
3. Love Letters	28
4. FlatLine	47
5. Revival	63
6. A Dedication For The Cool	85
7. Brown Skin Power	110
8. Bonus	128

INTRODUCTION

Seven chapters, seven poems each, and a bonus. The number seven is pure as it is recognized as a Godly number and relates to the spiritual connection with the universe. Imagine, your favorite memoir or coming of age story. Naima means 'God has given.' God has given me the privilege of living this life and experiencing all the wonders and the awesomeness, the upheavals, the pains and the joys life has to offer. Each poem is, of course, a piece of my heart and soul.

This is a memoir that hopefully touches your heart as the reader. The poetry defines and is supported by letters, words and lines that carefully hold the coming of realization--a new point in age that beckons the beginning of change. From the somber tones of failure to the rising triumphs, I stood in many points of my life where the turns were not clear. Decisions were not easy and I waited for someone or something to save me.

This collection of poetry will take you through emotions of love, self-discovery, abuse, illness, tackling the hardest parts of myself and doing my best with the cards I've been dealt. My belief is that our experiences are not just for ourselves, they are for others as well. Since I began writing as a little girl, my hope was

INTRODUCTION

that my work will start conversations. I want my vulnerability and the way I use my creative voice for transparency will inspire others to do the same.

Writing this book was not only therapeutic, it was challenging. Imagine being completely naked. That is how I was with a blank page. I allowed the words to disrobe the unseen, the words I haven't said and was pushed to say. I chose seven as the theme and titled this book *Pure* because I went through so many stages where I had to purge my toxins and cleanse. My poetry identifies with each of those times. This book is pure and raw with the truth of my true essence.

Crescendo is a poem that details my battles with mental illness and what it felt like to feel a total loss of self-control. It courses through the anger and the fear I had knowing that I have something, I could never outgrow or change. Battling illness is not easy and I truly had to redefine who I was as a person and as a woman.

Linguistic Lyrics is a coming of age poem. The moment I was forced from an adolescent to a young woman. Why this poem had to make the book is, I discuss the upheavals of being abandoned, then being loved by two parents and the pain I felt watching the highs and lows of my parents and the effect that had on me and my perception of love and the value of life and children. Wanting to be a sound board for women and letting every little girl know that scars are just reminders of where we have been and we can always kiss them better when they begin to itch.

She Smiled is a poem about a battle I was having with myself. Coming on the other side of the new woman I had to become and wanting to just breathe. Tired of feeling bogged down by the things I could not change, wanting to not be sad and filled with angst and pain. I just wanted to smile and let the breeze brush my skin and feel how beautiful the sun is and remind myself that I am full of light and special.

INTRODUCTION

Throwaway Love Remix, is a poem that I literally remixed to show that sometimes you throw love at the right person and they throw it back at you in a positive way. Love doesn't have to be painful or one sided it can be reciprocal and beautiful between two people. Love can be explored in all its phases, at all levels and transformed into power.

Super Hero reminded me of how human my parents are and that we cannot idolize them or anyone. Super heroes are only for comic books. Not to say I do not love my parents, because I truly do, but the truth of the matter is when we grow up, we suddenly realize how not so different we really are. This poem meant a lot to me to write because though it is my perspective, I think others can certainly relate.

Kick Ass Bitch, is a poem I wrote to revive myself. A reminder that all I have been through has made me special and resilient. To keep all things in perspective and never forget how powerful I actually am. I love this poem because I found myself in some really low places in the last couple of years. So, to have thought of a poem that recognizes the darkness and the light, is a positive way to turn failures into wins.

The Greatest Boy, is a dedication to my son. This identifies how I view myself as a mother, but most importantly, how I view him. It is a poem that will carry him through his youth till the time he is a grown man. My son means the world to me and having a chapter, entitled "Dedication for the Cool," would not be complete with a special piece

for him. My son is the most special part of me because he is a piece of me and I will forever cherish him.

You Can't Say Shit, is a poem to empower Black people. Reminding the world of our struggles and the oppression we constantly face. I think that the conversations need to held continuously. I chose this book to express that because of how it affects me on a daily basis. My perspective and how I see the world and how I hope to influence the people. My hope is that when white people read this book as well, they can empathize with our experience and look at themselves and how they can be the change that we all should want to see.

Baby I Often, is a gentle love poem, I placed it as a bonus because love is constant. Love should be experienced as much as possible. This poem celebrates my love and how thankful I am for him. It shows how I don't shy away from the strength love gives. I hope to always experience and explore the depth of love with my partner.

As previously mentioned, my hope is that God uses me and my voice to be an inspiration and inspire you as the reader, to have the gumption to share your stories and hopefully help someone else. Let's pass this on and let's press on. Welcome to Pure and may you be led to purity.

ACKNOWLEDGMENTS

I want to take this opportunity to acknowledge some people in my world. I could not get to where I am today alone. I have been blessed with a very distinct and special tribe that matter more to me than words can express. But since we are here, I am taking this moment to pour it all out.

First, I would like to acknowledge my parents. They have shielded me and truly pushed me to explore all that I am. Not only have they given me unconditional love, they helped me to see how special dreams can be and just how they can be achieved. I am thankful for my mother, Jennifer Garden Lovett; my step-father, Leon Lovett. These are the people that helped to mold me into the woman I am today and have given me the support and drive to not "dumb down" my voice, but to bring it all the way out.

Second, I would like to thank my uncle Luis Bernard. From an early age, he noticed the light in my eyes when I would speak and write. The conviction I had behind my words but most importantly, my thirst for wanting to write. Wanting to keep my words raw and pure. He has always supported my goals as a writer and have done so by showing up and leading me to opportunities to strengthen my writing and performance. He has graduated from mentor to uncle in my life and I am blessed that our paths have crossed. I am blessed to have the assurance of knowing, that I will always know him.

Next, I would like to thank my son, Lenox Roberts. He has been such a pillar in my life since the moment he was born. I have always wanted to be the best mother I could be for him. I have always wanted to pour love and light over him and let him know that he came here with so much love, power and light to share with the world. Having him as a son has taught me so many things and achieving my dreams is a must, in light of him.

I would like to thank my partner and best friend Quentin J. Hammonds. I cannot imagine this world without you and I am so thankful that we are in each other's life. You have taught me many things: patience, diligence and effectiveness in how to achieve are just a few. Not that I didn't already have these lessons but you helped me to fine tune them. Your love and support are a guiding light, the way you have held my hand through all the ups and downs, trials, tribulations, laughter and smiles--I am eternally grateful.

Last, but certainly not least, I would like to thank Dominique Glisson, my editor and friend. She has helped to mentor me through the process of publishing this special book and I am extremely grateful for our friendship and partnerships in business. It means a lot to have a good friend to cheer you on, but what makes this even more special is we root each other on.

To all I have acknowledged here, thank you from the bottom of my heart. There are so many more that I am thankful for but these especially, I hold dear and I could not have seen myself through to the end of this experience with this book, *Pure*, without you.

Chapter One
IN A HEARTBEAT

Nature Freestyle

The white smoke dressed in the vapors--

Of fog rose slowly over the rhythm

Of the river in the morning rise of the sun glaze.

The remnants of the night

Lingered with the lowering of a crisp

Full moon White and textured

It felt so close with closed eyes

Imagined my fingers grazing the

Crevices of the night planet,

The thoughts ran like shooting stars

At the speed of light, the notion of Nature

Comforted the space that left me naked

Constantly enveloped in the

Peace of the equivalent to the certainty

I just yearned for the ability to be

Unequivocally Free by definition

Of freed, then and now...

Freedom

She Smiled

The day seemed to

Begin with the stretching

Of arms that pulled at the sides

Of the ribcage the day was bright the water

glistened as if to have stars in them,

She saw her reflection

Tasting the salty waters

Cleansed her tongue

In likeness with her skin She smiled

Feeling the beat of the sun

That lifted the golden tones

In the melanin that clothed her

She listened to the call of the

Spirit beyond the surface of

Anything tangible, the acute

Ear she had let her heart beam

IN A HEARTBEAT

As bright as the sun rays that

Touched down to highlight her footsteps

She smiled; taken into account the

Drops of tears that ran away

With the depth of the sea

There were no more sorrows here

Missing you tomorrows or beckoning

the Beg of a hug or hand to tug at the loss

That wounded the soul

She smiled; standing corrected

By the several detours that

Kept her bewildered about the man

Cries that seemed to fall on

Deaf ears to the rejection

Of anything that seemed

Down right human--she

Was leaving it buried

She smiled; no more waiting

For calls from imaginary

Friends, no more waiting

For soften-rough hands

No more doubting Self loathing

And powder-like Fears that just

Seemed to keep her dusted

No more drowning in the guilt

Of things not worth lingering

Holding on to a shadow

That had hopscotch in the background

She smiled

Unhinged She smiled Open Loud

Laughter floating

In the air like the ringing Of song

She smiled

So brightly, till her cheeks hurt

She kept the smile wide so her

Son could join in the joy she

Radiated like a bright queen

Which reflected in the sea that

She greeted her words were heard

Cleansed and preserved

As all feelings are worth acknowledging

But none of us should

keep our souls in bondage

Exhale, release, smile

Just as she did.

Smile.

How High

This morning I sit high Amongst the beauty

In the blue skies and fluffy White clouds.

The suns brightness

Lightened the golden dust in the

Corners of my eyes I feel

So highly favored and preserved

To live life loudly, lovely

Comforted and blessed by

God's hand Love, perseverance

Kindness and beauty, I wanted to take

A minute to write while sitting in this plane

While contemplating on the

higher power The happiness

I share with those I love

Near or far the tears that

Swell among my pupils

As confirmation, deep rooted

thoughts of evolution Happiness,

Time and space where

I dwell Awareness, our connection

That is ever growing

And forever strengthening.

So I contemplate think and ask, how high...

Press On

Today was challenging
Feeling unwell and losing
A grip on the real space
I was occupying Lost
Having to refocus my energy Hanging
on by a thread
The depths of my emotions Consumed
me to never
Ending spaces of depression
Falling quickly and anxiously
Unable to keep from slipping
Like water to oil, I was tripping
In dripping pain
Productive yet deepens in the well Of
unnerving,
This day I am feeling the strain
In my eyes and feeling undeniably
Constrained
The thoughts flow
In the vein of negativity
Keeping the mind
In a bind
It's hard to stay positive
When you're constantly being attacked

Overwhelmed by the present

Take deep breaths Ready

Go One

Two

Three

Four

Five

Press on

Poetry

Jump Hover

Push to overcome

Learn and accept

Overturn and provide

Step forward, link to home

Bystanders dare to cease

Progression

Overwhelmed push through

Health concerned push through

Making

All Choices

Power

Respect

Ownership

Believe

Accept

Praise God Ase

Power

Pulled by gravity of a wind song and c

hime to a line A color to a sublime

We're calling hustlers to a time

Of revived lives

In passion twist

To power trip in a wandering

Mind we must act like the blind

And relive through the touch of Braille

Our stories hold weight

Tons of our stories can heal Or destroy

Impeccable hope to

Provide the power to inspire

Power to ignite the potential deep

Within, heal many ideas of

Never having such

Believe and trust God to transform

Your energy, reach high,

High above to the

Most High Keeping the

heart and soul aligned

Invite your power to no end

Believe in yourself

There is power in your fight

To evolve continuously

We are ever growing

And More, we embrace

Powerful we become.

The Rolling Hills

Greet the ground As if to swallow

The paths of many The endless road

Tells tails of whispered

Dreams and unhinged trials

That compliment the toughness

Of the rocky edges to Paradox

The blacktop, the highlights, the

White lines, the blacktops endless

Elite to greater.

Traveling alongside a road with no worries

Or barricades for danger to

Plummet the woes of broken souls at

Clinched fist of life's grip.

How powerful is the control

Of freedom in sea of open space

And air that's stifled by the caged lies

Of troubled water the space hasn't been

Blessed to be baptized in

Waves of water pebbles

To quench the thirsty roots of dying expectancies,

The black and white leaves no

Room for slated grey where

Questions and doubt kiss like lovers

In a midst of a chaotic sea of unfolding desires

That swallow the crying soul on the rolling hills

Of an endless road and parted

Crevices shifted by plateaus and crustaceans

Layers much like the image of a lonely girl on an

Open space with no sides to maintain the colors in

The fabric of her skin...

Torn back, the black and white force

The shadow of a divide

Ties longing for the heat of the

Sunshine and the rays of glistening light

To highlight the curves in an

Upside-down smile

Who left her yearning for the comfort

frozen in childhood innocence

Mirrored the self in an abandoned road.

The lanes are endless the highlighted

dotted white lines are not enough black

to depict the

Majority and still we stand still in the center

Of black and white

With pain splattered on concrete

The only red that oozes is the flow

when the skin is cut and even then,

even then it's all

black and white roads to endless journeys,

Greeted by tortured desires.

Waiting, waiting on the peace to find me

in the midst of rolling hills and dark areas

to be another image in the midst of stamped concrete

instead let these footsteps talk loudly for me.

Chapter Two

BLUE BLACK PURPLE

Linguistic Lyrics

Letting Linguistic lyrics bless this paper

Bleed blue, calming playful and always innocent

Black confused, yet still mindful

And purple, personal evolution

And maturity

And wisdom beyond my own

However the wind blows

And how I feel it in my soul

My colors change on the mood

Adopting a different shade

That seems to color all of

My personalities, convey change and my realities

Perform my ranging soul

And builds mountains around my curiosities

So discernment and maturity

Could be transparent

Reveal my wounds and battle scars

That only seem to show my growth

Unveil my fears mixed with vulnerability

Erase my innocents and moving gracefully

Into adulthood and now

The metamorphoses is completed

And I became a woman

Building my own thoughts

Feeling comfortable in my own skin

As one may say

Proud and ready to take

On the steps toward

Knowing more about me

Taking journeys in

My mind as I rewind the wheels

Of time and praise

God for a life In turbulence mixed with stability

Planted views and structure in the

Midst of pain and hurt

Watching my mother clinically depressed

And suicidal wasn't a dream, it was reality

But her love for her newborn gift from God Saved her

Evolving into a revolutionary woman

And a survivor from torment and abuse

And moving in her own life to find herself

Peaceful and happy

This is why I write

To strip the covers off of the truth

Express constructive rhythmic words

That seem to hit the hearts core

I spit the truth arresting the mind

Into each metaphoric syllable

Capturing similes and pumping

It into your veins like a vaccine

Wait...

Take time to really hear my words

Dancing for joy at three

I can still feel the pounds

Of the goat skins in my chest

Waving my hands mimicking a dance

For a ceremony was the only bond to a father

I don't know...

Performing arts is our only connection

Never sincerity or true words

Just on-going disappointments

And constant craters forming

Bigger than the ozone

So in a whirlpool

Of drowning unknown memories

And deep cut wounds, I still find Peace,

But I'm too young at three

To know all the details

Yet I know, God sees my pain and my hurt

Knows that not one man

can undo the biological

Father and daughter process

So in turbulence mixed with stability

Planted views and structure in the midst of pain

And hurt then the only father I know

Teaches a young girl who he doesn't know

Out of love for her spirit and the love

He holds for her mother

Took the role and made it his own

And knew he was going to love me unconditionally

And he is... my father

Praise God because now I know

True love and I lived in a two-parent

Home, at nine years old

I knew the importance and value

Behind it

Isn't it funny how little children

Know more than adults sometimes?

I said isn't it funny how little

Children know more than adults sometimes?

Fast forwarding to the present

Hearing the deep blues of young girls

Who experienced what I did

Or maybe worse

Scars cannot be undone or even healed

They are always there to remind us of

Where we've been

Some sistas are still walking their path

Wondering when the lights gonna shine

Wondering when the lights gonna shine

Wondering when the lights gonna shine

I stand before you hoping that my words

Can be of some inspiration so another

Can take it and teach another

You know, each one teach one

This is why I write

The spoken word is inevitable

Making me believe that any and everything

Is possible taking my mind

Into deep meditations just so

I can listen to my heart beat

And having conversations that

Never begin or end focusing

On thoughts that you and me

Haven't even pondered yet

Hoping that my thoughts can have

That Impact or maybe more

Creating painted murals just like

The biblical stories just to show the truth

It's funny what colors the heart can bleed

Is it...

Blue

Black

Or

Purple?

I think this poem shows all three.

Crescendo

Inevitably Swooped off my feet

A leaf in a windstorm

Rooted once as a tree

Ripped to plummet

I--a mere piece in a tsunami

This the essence of a life

I buried scripted poems in my

Veins Hoping they would write me

A new lifeline Called out to

God with painful Cries

And disappearing diamonds in my eyes

I once glistened while my smiles lit up

Like The sun now somber and dismayed

Uneasy unsure.

The brink of a new version of self-

Unsure or ready to relinquish her

Reaching ions for the sanctity of my sanity

The overwhelming brain transfers of

The fear of actually going insane

Waiting for the main to tame the maintain

Slipping essence of her like

water slips through rocks Naima,

the woman of strength

And power

The woman of hope and positivity

Falling into the suction of depression

The upheavals of anxiousness flowing

Over my body like tidal waves

Push and pull, push and pull

The waters aggressive like hurricanes

Washed up ashore no rest on assurance

This is what it feels like to die

The person you once knew dies

Slip and fall, struggling to gain footing

There is no ground to step on

Last long, the sad song on repeat

Fall, fall deep into the consciousness

Of unconscious wanting to be free

Free like a jaybird in beauty of blue

Wisps with wings from tree to tree

Leaf to leaf, twig to twig

Twinging at the sound of my own voice

Shaking as if to have

Parkinson's or that of a junky

Coming down in cold sweats

The sound of cackling and crashing verbs

And words from tones of others

Erupting emotions rising like the

Height of mountains

Busy streets passing the eardrums like trucks

In a car cash or screeching sound of

Nails on a blackboard

Reacting to the point of seclusion.

Agoraphobia Pushed feelings that froze

My steps to set Foot on the pavement

Forget 10 toes down

Keep me safe in the comfort

of familiar territory Home.

Home became the prison I hid,

In prison in my own

Mind running, running

Vigorously out of time.

Passion drowned in the depths of the sea

Slipping from my grasp.

Edgy depression keeping

All senses submerged in a dark hole

Numb the outcry fell on deaf ears

Hands of care swept off my back

Nothing but the feeling of the wind

Air wasn't strong enough to dry tears on the inside

Tears fell often,

Collecting in a puddle beneath

My bed large enough to bathe in

Hoping the bath would replenish my soul

Dying and being conformed

I felt the voice inside me as loud as

God Bellowed out wanting to hear again

Accept, accept the new you my daughter

Defenseless and fearful

Seconds, minutes from dying

This is the onslaught of a never-ending spiral

Doing your best to find the grip of an invisible rail

Spinning, spiraling out of control no explanation

For the tremors and tripping, panic, the static

The inability to hear past the brink of shaking

The body reacts like being triggered

By electric shock Locked into a

State of unbelievable fear keep me grounded.

Lifted up, Up so high the stakes are high

Boom the bottom hits like bricks

Stick to the flows that remind

You of home.

Lost a long way from home.

Accept what, how can I...

I have to remember to survive

The lift was that of a crescendo.

Not Worth The Distance

I Shouldn't Need A Passport For What The Most High

HasAlready Made Domestic For Me,

Neither Should You Question My Unconditional Love

Yet You Only Seem To See Me With

Lazy Eyes Medical Chronic Illness

Called Dislike Is Only A Gateway

To A Disease Called Hate

I wondered how the withering of charm

Chokes the space of forever

I wondered how I ever fell

For your kind eyes and handsome face

Welcoming smile,

Typical tall, dark and handsome

The disguise you walked in shielded in

The Stench of darkness

Lack of compassion

Where love never grew

Fears deepen with the raise of

Abusive hands

Words that shattered

Everything I thought

My life threatened 10 times over

The cover of care

Never there Constant danger

My screams were stifled

Under your intimidation

Your relentless will to torture

Fear consumed me

Trauma followed me

Stalked by your shadow

Pounded concrete with

Quick feet and hid on

Subway trains and filthy streets

Escape wasn't an option

Boxed in,

Unworthy, I would say Not special,

I would say Not beautiful,

I would say Not loved,

I would say The negative Transformed everything

There was no escaping

Haunting dreams and calls

That kept tremors as comfort Fear as safety

Yearning for the rescue from a nightmare

I laid awake in a never-ending nightmare

Hate visited my bedside

Seeped into the depths

Of the subconscious

It took everything not to consider

Causing your expiration

The days I desired forever love

Love didn't live here

Love would never grow here

As my belly grew with life

The mission of yours

Was a suction cup, sucking Life from my veins

The saving grace

Was the birth of my newborn

Gift from God

My son saved me

Saved me from an abuser

Saved me from a vampire

Saved me from death

Saved his momma in love

Then, is when I realized

You were never worth the distance

You Damn Right

You Damn Right

Ain't Nothing About This Counterfeit,

But for Some Reason

You're Too Scared to Cash In

The Most High is the Teller...

And Even With All The Love

I'm Depositing You Still End

Up Bankrupt So I'm a

Withdraw From This,

Save What Little Bit

I Can of You Before I Overdraft...

Then I'll Just Be

Exactly What You Want Me To Be...

A Traveler's Check in Your Safe

Swing

Hellos don't swing low and hit roots

Like goodbyes do

Hellos don't swing low and brush cheeks

Like goodbyes do

Hellos don't bury deep and take root

Like goodbyes do

Hellos don't make room and

Cause smiles and faded frowns

Like goodbyes do

Hellos don't shake hands and pocket chances

Like goodbyes do

Poets don't say hello, they linger

Paint on white pages and stain areas,

Not Like goodbyes do

Just Need To Say

With the cold

Shivers greet my core

Speaking to the tingling fingers

That frost from the bite of

Freezing temperatures,

Inside fridges the depth of unsung

Truth has spawn forever

Shivers inside like horrid space within

I wish I could be set free

Instead captive to the undying shiver

The frost from the bite of burning

Desire to seek the fine

Once felt to conquer

To overcome beyond 'ok'

But to be excellent and travel

The lengths of Go rather than

Stay- Feeling like the same has to be

The difference of a forever dream

Just want to be shaken awake

To feel anything but numb

Free Write

This morning is cold and

Brisk with the bare trees and

Blanket gray skies that lend

The break of water drops through

Broken clouds.

Chapter Three
LOVE LETTERS

Throw Away Love-Remix

Black sun kissed Dripping melanin

Lined magenta walls

Of Complied, Contorted Contemplations on

My symmetrical movements through,

Padded souls and fallen stones

By the sight of my diamond eyes

And confident attitude

Heart as big as the ocean

Sista was known for throwing away love

You know, the sexy kind,

That would Devour your mind

With my presence

Stop the time...

Eastern, Western, Central and Pacific

Sticking to my brown sugar skin like glue

Discussing everything from over

The rainbow to the news

Toes curling in ribbons and smiles

Climbing the Eiffel Tower

Of mental ecstasy Tasting my essence

We became each other's secret diary

Each stroke of the pen

To a blank page was

An invaluable counter For sustenance for

The parched souls

We encase, we became Like the blind

When apart, re-lived

Through the touch of time in Braille

Felt us, souls meshed

With blessed hands

Longing for the complimentary

Addition to a new chapter Holding on to each other's

Spirit like purified quicksand

Dried tears and bottled ties

Baggage heavy like miles,

5,000-mile trip the golden dust in each other's

Eyes we discovered a true

Reflection that beckoned

The depths of crystal clear- Waterfalls

I recognized that men throw love around,

Just as women do

Uncertain and making everything so

Certain with no room to discover

Just claiming a stake and a place

Because right now it feels oh so good

Knowledge is power type shit

That I'll fight for what's right

We are revolving-

Familiar as if

We always had each other

Eclipsing anatomies converse secretly

We inched closer, closer and closer

Saying; do you feel me yet?

We got our shit together, type love

We'll do anything just to secure

The smile, hug and kiss

The difference here is

The feeling of being still

And feeling the exhale of

A deep breath- let go-

Yours viciously immersed into

LOVE LETTERS

The twinkling pavements Drawing the bond as if

To draw a bath we Were doused in the

Splendor that our presence

Greets us with when together

Nothing and everything matters

Right now, I stopped the time

For you, made space in the

Crowded chamber of my heart where

Sorrow and scorched

Wounds already controlled it

Put all these thoughts

Into this knapsack of stars and told you

To eat from it slowly

In turn you offered

Me yours

We both Were finally fed

Chose this lifetime To intertwine

Making every day The first day of

Christmas Combined with Valentine's Day

And make the cherry on top

ME

We locked eyes Butterflies followed

Crowded the pit of my belly

Where we were stagnant,

We raised each other

Silent tones Raging emotions

You come before I open my eyes And before they shut

Sista like me was known-

For throwing away love

The silence It use to creep into my bed

And Sleep with me recklessly

Echoing sounds From your voice box Through the phone

And it seemed Like words

And I glided on the midnight blue sky

With stiletto heels

You heard me

Felt me Said yes

Weightless Senseless Sleepless

No convincing

Love always lived

With us It's God.

It's knowing

I am your woman,

Chosen

You are my man

Kissing my spirit Like fairytale dreams

You urge me to dig deeper

Feel deeper and stand up on ya,

You got my back

Better than a stiff rock

I love you, I know you

Altogether adore you

I'll be wonder woman

And tell you to recite

My name into the wisps

Of the wind

Finally, I am in control

Enough to checkmate the game and remain

Queen

See Sista like me was

Known for throwing away love

Now I embrace it

Endure it No evasion

Just devotion

Empowered Evolution to become stronger

Between you and I

Healed wounds

On the bottom of my feet

Where I burned holes

Tight roping passion

With the wrong kinds

Where boys stay playing

On swing sets and Pissing in sandboxes

He appreciates true beauty

Something so real

It's bigger than the universe

They cowered at the diamonds In my eyes

He stood to understand each

Gem that made me glisten

Energized by our combined

Impeccable determination

No more painful lies

Our I love you's

Stick like our sun kissed

Birth-fits

Not letting go

Embracing

love

In

Paradise

Tangled Like Silly String

Wrapped, entangled in key

substances to loving you

Harvesting chips of you

As if to have a reserve to

Keep me nourished,

Sipping from your words

To keep me hydrated in

Everything that is you,

I am resting on everlasting.

Ever pleasurable,

Ever patient,

Ever gentle,

Kind to the sublime, your love has been

Gifted by the highest,

I am grateful to

Receive it and reverse it, for rough times.

Bottling it up deep inside,

Your love is like Velvet to my soul,

Greeting me in the morning,

Kissing my golden-brown skin

Existing in places, no other can.

Enveloped by your key notes,

Pacing the rhythms in

Your breath along with the beats

Of our hearts, synced,

As if a perfect design for a match.

I love the language we speak in silence

Swept in the steady breath,

Listening to the lines unspoken with our hearts

The next words we utter would be in unison

Then laugh, and jokingly state

"Get out of my head."

Instantly, in that moment between

The last word uttered and the

Short silence thereafter we both agree

There is no place better than where we are.

For You I Will

I Wish You Could See

How Thankful I Am

How Much You Mean

To My Spirit

Your Lyrics Create a Better Song

A New Melody That Compliments

My Lifeline...

I've Been Preparing Myself For The

"Will You be My Wife"

Line So I Can Be Honored To

I'm Yours & You're Mine

With the flickers of fire flies

That beat with the butterflies

In common they fly to the best part of the heart

Making the beginning and the end one in the same,

Blanket the true essence of endless

Light fills the highlights

Of the areas unseen

I'm pulling from the depths of the universe

Calling for the planets to show you how

Well you revolve around the spine of

Out of this world I'm reaching for the length

Of long awaited hug filled

With I miss you For you, For you will

I will reverse time

Just so I can have more hours More hours to love

More hours to say ours

And ours live beyond the test of time

Forever never felt so good

To say mine is the best

Lifeline and I'll trust You with all of it

You define everything

True love should be

What's for you is for me

Finally

For you

For you

I will do anything

Kisses

The day falls with The setting of the sun

We gaze at a sunset

Through bare windows

Suddenly the skies

Call on gray clouds Dribbles of rain

Kiss the window seal

Kisses ensue passionately

Hands flow across thighs

I'm getting high off

Your passion

My energy crashing

Against yours like waves in an ocean

The river flows between my thighs

I just require more kisses

You grip the nape of my neck

Pull me in deeper, closer

Tongues swirl My eyes greet the backs of my lids

Feeling the heat transfer From your body to mine

It was only a matter of time

No time to move, we are consumed

Moans and sounds fill the air

I beg for more kisses Kisses flow down my body

Around my breasts and nipples,

I love how you take it slow

Kisses fill me, engrossed

In your aura making me

Hum your name in

Sweet pastures Concerns of time

Place nor space and all others fall

The present is all we have

Kisses flow down my stomach

Around my navel

Drown me in kisses downtown

Oh how I love your kisses

Kisses make me feel

Special, wanted, craved

My passion higher

Beacons the freak in me

Let her out and run wild

Fill me up with all of your kisses

Loving Deep

I'm asking you to Never leave

I'm asking that We dream

I'm asking that

We soar above the clouds

I'm asking that we let our love

Echo beyond the universe

Among the stars we glisten

Keep us in the arms of God

We don't have nothing without love

The waring of the world

Is healed by our love

Let's survive and be revived

Time and time again through

The power of our love

I'm asking for you to allow me

To love you immensely

I'm asking you to never

Let me leave you

Cause earth shattering

Love to flow into the world

Make love to me deep

Deeply when things go array

Make love to me

Remind me that this love

Is forever with you

Make love to me

Cause us to never be blue

Make love to me

So we earthquake

The breaks for the sake Of forever

I'm asking that

We remember how powerful we are

I'm asking that we remember

The times I'm asking that we travel

Many times

Around the now the depth of our love

And fall repeatedly and never touch

The ground, afloat your love

This is comforting

This is worth surviving

This is worth celebrating

The blackness of our love

Is beauty and excellent

Love Finds Thee

Love inspires the fluid

Language of harp strings

For the way the heart sings

Dancing in the embrace of a wind song

Love beckons the notion of a brace

That is forever giving

And rising to the occasion

That supports change

Love is the beacon of light
Harboring the secrets at the pit
Of the soul of being
Lingering for the eternal kiss
Of forever.

Love, be a match struck by
Gold of flickering flame
Too out of control to ever hose down
Instead we hold down the
Moment-to-moment magic
Only time and seconds can acquire

Love is the fire that never dies
And the pain that follows
Are the struggle blocks to motivate
Growth to an invested milestone
Introduced by the onset of birth

Love is freedom in flight Of fearless chance that
Never declines but catches the
Very being exposed by a destined forever

And that is relieved.

Love requires the constant inquiry
Of truth backed by a soft blockade
Of a daring desire to stay hidden

Love should be unwrapped transparency
To request a soul dance and a sun shower
To celebrate the flames in standing
Ovation for the privilege of beauty

Love should be both admired and embraced
And never shadowed by a facade
of blanked--Pure
Love is everything gritty and bitter sweet
And powerfully life changing

Love swallowed me and submerged me
To dare to glare, to breathe, to greet, to love
Differently the moment I became a mother

Love Letter

Good Morning Q
I thought I would take my time
Write you a letter with you in mind

May your eyes feel swollen with

Warmth from the words you read

As you see, this is my love letter

To you, I hope you receive it well

May it fill you up like water

From a well, excavate my soul

To fill with pure sunshine

And the scent of roses

A flood overwhelms me

Except I dare not drown

I'm saved in your heart

You take up so much space

In mind as if you packed up and moved in

The world surrounds and I swear

All I hear and see is you

Colors warm like autumn

Swarming thoughts more than you

Can fathom, stand in love with me

And let's make the galaxies jealous

As we orbit like Orion

I'm loving you through kind eyes

And melting colors from flickering

Butterflies,

This is my love letter to you

LOVE LETTERS

I hope you receive it well

Let it not get lost in transit

Or in translation feel the depth

Of my love through this blank Page,

we travel many stages

Each is an incredible performance

A longing for the everlasting

The fuel sparks transfer

Like spark plugs to forever

We charge up and power up

No lines to play with no games

To encounter just serving up

These flames that

Spark equally

Your sound be like music

To a soul break

Each time you're near, my heart

Flutters--it's like my soul wakes

Stay so I'm rejuvenated like

Power cords and solar energy

Stay so I can breathe freely

And wings can span into safety

I mean stay cause my laugh

Sounds better with yours

Stay cause if we breathe deep,

We can actually listen

To the heart's rhythm,

That begs to submit

We come up with plans to forever

Though the present has the time

Tied up in unclosed doors

Anxiously giving a sense of

All the space to where we

Revitalize the spirit down

We the same thunder and the same

Wave with distinct compliments

For how we celebrate

Love, I'm drawing closer let

This never asunder

This is my love letter,

write me Back soon...

Love always,

NYI

Chapter Four
FLATLINE

Naked

They asked her to show up

Bare

Exposed

No armor

Just as you are

Unwired Unhinged

Just open Receptive

Willing Submissive Unapologetic

As long as you don't--

Sway too loud

They asked you to come unannounced

Calling all that is, with your

-- Piercing eyes

A stance that signifies--

I am not messing around

They asked you to come silenced

And loud in how you SLAY

They asked you to come bare.

Yet...Who?

Who is worthy enough to

Embrace your nakedness?!

      Superhero

When growing up

You had the speed of flash

The power of superman

The wrath of hulk

Spun circles in webs like

Spider man and had the healing

Power of vibranium

You were everything great

And mighty in my eyes,

There was nothing you could

Do wrong and no flaws to follow

As children we idolize Our parents

Commend them and fall to their every

Demand

They caution us to be careful

Not to forget our place

They rear us into the people

We become

All things are provided

And nothing can be done wrong

They keep us safe and sound

We become adults

To be shocked

That our parents

Are no different from who we are

They struggled with finding their way

They observed the road in which way to turn

They placed their feet on shaky ground

They denied assistance when they needed aid They

made mistakes and took some

Secrets to the grave

They begin to tell us things they hid in darkness You

begin to look at them with a different set of eyes And

the super hero you knew

Was nothing short Of just human

Break Open

Shatter like a Glass fixture

Break open Like a coconut

Break open and Let all that is

Hang and air dry

Speak loud

And question all the things

That's tugging at ya

I sat and cringed at the

Idea that the man I thought

Loved me used me like washed up wood

I watched the woman I thought was,

My best friend, betray me and

Kiss my husband's ass behind my back

I filtered through the unseen

And used my intuition to guide me

Through the rest

This pitiful ass motherfucker

Caused a rupture inside me

Dared to hold my hand and lead

Me deeper into the darkness

Filling my insides up with black coal

Becoming an ice box at the pit of my core

He traveled distances over roads

Longed for more big butts and thighs

Faded smiles and sparkling eyes

Fell deeper into immature habits

I played the fiddle to the fool

Thought he was just wanting me more

Craving for more of me but in actuality

He was craving to be noticed, desired

And seen by any woman who paid him

Attention but me

He paid for it like going broke

On expensive habits

He couldn't afford

Let this air out like dirty laundry

Air out and expose the depth

Of disgust you caused me

And tears you encouraged

Splatter and fall and break The fuck open

I pitied this fool
Who was lost like a
Child without guidance
Lost like a puppy without a home

I stood by and felt the wrath
Of a dried-up boy yearning to be a
man, I watched and engulfed
The stench of rotting heart
And delve deeper into a darkness
A place I've never been wandering
And lost in unfamiliar territory
I gave my life for you
Breathed life into a union you spat on
This was all a game like the
Olympics And you juggled the turn of every sport

I drowned and longed for a man to love me
Need me, instead of criticize me, instead
Of resent me for being a woman of substance
Jealousy doesn't only run through women
Men can be the biggest players and for me,
I had no idea
I desired a place where only a man and wife dwell

FLATLINE

Too bad I was digging a hole

And falling down a dried up well

The pain I felt was like that of a truck

I kept things deep inside my gut

On the outside, I smiled while my marriage

Was falling apart

I dare not utter the words

That made feel like I was in shambles

Alone and isolated feeling useless

And unloved my heart broke open

And blood oozed like an infected wound

I fell down deep, in an ongoing spiral

He found comfort in a Louisiana swing

Kept his affairs hidden for long periods of time

Until the day he was exposed like bare skin

She was no better than him

They played house while being promised

To separate partners

Wandered around in secret and even

Spent time over spilled wine and

Dirty sheets, he was so filthy

And she was just as unclean

I scored more information

More than I wanted to know

She, his fiancé and though

They were both already wed

I wondered what these two had to gain

Or why break hearts as if it were a game

Marriage is nothing to play with

He took it seriously for all of two minutes

And I just soaked up the efforts that

Were all one-sided

I hated to feel... Numb, I was, this was the end

And I was abandoned

What felt like for the 100th time

See you can be left in so many ways

The man I thought would prove me

Wrong, that men always leave

Just added to my long-kept theory

Here we are at the end of this time

It all broke open at the drop of a dime

Pull It Up

I woke up completely lost

My body was new and

I felt I lost all my words and

Everything I knew was ruined

My steps were deformed, unknown spaces

My smile wasn't crooked but misplaced

Or out of space or unfound

I tried to tailor my steps to fit a disguise

Some days, the harder I tried, the more I failed

To communicate this isn't easy at all

But this is a part of my story

Where I survived a fall

I took in the idea of never

Being the same and the more

I pushed the harder it became

Acceptance wasn't something

I could Do, I traveled journeys in my mind Trying

to completely redesign

The maze I was in--figuring Something had to give

I carefully transformed the test

Of time when moving was impossible

I went places in my mind

Once doing for myself was more of a chore

Then regularly convenience

Or something out of love

I coursed the places inside where

I would hide There was no way to define myself, for

I felt left behind

You might ask

What is this that you see

What does all of this really mean

To carefully put it and boldly

State to make this pure

It would be worthy to say

I suffered deeply with depression you see

Anxiety consumed me and

I didn't know what to do

I fell, and fell deep inside,

I had to pull myself up From the flat line

Title Me Why

The inability to lay rest on a decision, post, pause on

Movement and development of a desired, romance,

Pin shots on past torment; lay dormant on the inside of

Parasite, boxes feeding mutating

Emotions of repetitious actions

FLATLINE

I hold on, standing side-by-side,

Folding more, yet still stiff,

Strong enough

Not to kneel without the definition

Of being one and only.

Camera lenses behind recorded memories,

Where I swore

I'll lay down my life for love,

Etch it on the insides of my womb,

With the creation of a life,

And raise it beating to the sound of unity,

I got Junkie track scars trailing towards

Dismembered places,

From the hit of a man, the high of the illusion

Of co-existing in a smile

And a laugh, regardless if

It was borrowed, because in the end,

we all return To sender, so I endure the hurt,

her tears left on my chest cavity and cradle Soaked pillowcases in my arms,

clink-tight like locked suitcases,

Yeah Move On

His story is always over mine,

So they become historical artifacts

That often imitates the future,

verbal exchange that almost instantly

Ends up in a demolishment,

Of everlasting, ever listening,

Every growing, ever standing

Ever mutates to never,

vastly like 21st century weather,

Forgetting we stuck together, soft,

Gentle like cotton clouds, sweet like cotton candy,

Heated spice, too unique for thermometers

Seeking temperatures,

Two hearts shattered;

I refuse to be sheltered in convenient shadows

And held too special to seek the market for a better

compliment to my style

Flawless, yet flawed to be denied,

Claim me in broad daylight,

Dad said if he refuses,

Question his intent,

Because it's not one you seek

Bleak and numb, I lend,

Rent in my space

And get stuck with debts of unpaid, payments

All for the sake of broken

                Exhausted

FLATLINE

Feeling the strain through the fingernail beds.

Joining sentences on a strand of yawn...

Feet drag to the next step,

while muscles release like boiled spaghetti.

Exhausted

Keeping tabs on my slumber clock,

And my hours are not pulling dollars.

Falling, in a center of stress

Piled on the confines of my subjected reality...

Did I mention, I'm tired...

Holding the stick of denied

Doors and closed mouths when

I begged for assistance.

The system has whelped my back and keloids form

Braille for sake of rhetoric for memory...

Exhausted

Pumping 5 hour into my veins

Feeling the weights on my eyes

As my lids bench press... Caution, my fuse is short,

My patience is slim,

my voice is husky from lack of sleep

And chain smoke, position...

I'm waiting for a newness,

I'm yearning for the desires

when my heart sang.

I'm calling jackets from past comforts and bliss.

Bliss, where my cheeks leaked a hint of red,

where the company of a man amused me,

Feeling like I am a woman...

I'm numb to a routine...

Exhausted

Sleep, while walking...

Tampered, and hurt, Beaten and Alive,

Pieces of innocent pleasantries, remind me...

I skipped along a beach in my

Mind and licked the salt in a clear blue,

I remember a genuine hug,

And a kiss that followed with a smile,

Goodnight... I remember feeling

The sun on my brown skin in a banging

Sundress...

I simply think too much when I'm...

Exhausted

Rock

She packaged stores invested by renters.

Tailored thoughts of kisses to be savored.

Most memories become, remembrances

Of something she'll never savor.

Blink eyes, beyond her imaginations' locations.

Her only promise is forward progression.

Her passion is smooth yet textured

From character, she's developed in later chapters.

Her eyes swell with tears at times,

But never fall cause no one's there to capture.

She chases a memory that becomes distinct

Into haunting her realities.

Secretly, she still blames "he" for leaving her...

She only knew his hand for

guidance on romantic pathways

In hidden passages, she spoke vows that denigrated

In the whirlwind of adolescent behaviors.

Innocent, yet grown enough for promises;

Most adults make before biologically, they become unable...

. . .

Yeah, she hopes, dreams,

secretly plots her days around faces unseen.

Wondering if her dreams

Of a killer are those of the man she'll never meet...

Guess I can say, at least in darkness

She'll never be lonely, because herself and I,

She is the gatekeeper...

I'll rock her heart And cradle her to sleep...

Sleep...

Don't weep

Just....Unjustly, sleep, peacefully....

Chapter Five
REVIVAL

Visions

Kept the lyric in a bubble wrap

Rehearsed the experience like

The same way the feelings wore on me

Like a drawn-out stress signal

Loved the romance wrapped up in

The sweet of how the heart struggled to push

Past the junk mail

The power tripped shockwaves and the cloudy

Smudge that challenged the

Glimmer of a lit possibility for change

When the stolen moments and preyed

On vulnerability were all means

To survive the darkness of broken, Slated concrete

Where the flesh on the left side of my face was bitten by

The moisture of the cold

Ground and tarnished hands

That masked to give anything

More than a blanket of love

It just don't go deep enough

It just don't reach deep enough

It just don't match a word in a light

Footstep and disappearing trials

We act, we move, we entice, we entrance

And hold onto the comfort of a painful

Memory that requires something more than

Surface and played up a dream

A whimsical fantasy which didn't

Invite the reality to take a seat in forever

Kick Ass Bitch

Picked up the broken Pieces and etched them

In like attachments To my crown

Giving definition to the fact

That I am and forever will be a gem

Tears fell like pearls Dried on cheeks as

A reminder even my tears Are beautiful

REVIVAL

Redefining the woman, I am
And pulling from the depths of my soul
That I am the definition of special

Special like the light in the sky from
Midnight stars
Special like the birth of newborn child
Special like the beauty of the wonders of the world
Special like any edifice you would marvel after

Wanting my voice to
Echo instead of fade in the distance
Realizing my desire to live
Outweighed my feelings to die
This won't beat me

Tilting the devils attempt to defeat
All that was and all that ever will be
Giving a stand-up fight
Toe-to-toe like Creed
There is no giving in There is no other way
But to face this and overcome it
Strong like the mother who Bared a child
Had a c-section

And marched back into the classroom

To complete her masters

Strong like the woman

Who battled the court system

Systematic abuse and the abuse

Of a worthless man and won

Strong like the woman who

Endured the rejection of

Love from a worthless Husband who left

My laundry out

For others to try on a piece

Of my clothing as if I ain't human

Strong like the definition of the many

Ancestors that taught me to march on

Keep my head high and never turn a blind eye

Strong like the woman who battled

Depression and anxiety

And conquered her ability to sustain her mental health

The fight to be the best mother

The best woman

The best partner The best friend

The person I could ever be

I'm that woman, I'm that strong
So when I ever forget it,
I stare Myself square in the eye
And say
You are one
KICK ASS BITCH

Star Gaze-Freestyle

To fix my eyes on the tiny specs of light

That indicate bright to keep the darkness

Hopeful, allow myself to drift past the blanket

Of midnight I am engulfed by the mysterious

Space between time and infinite

The galaxy allows my fantasies to run rapid

Like the sky walker resting dreams

With the feeling of desire

And carefully plummeting the fears in a space

Landing where gravity remiss and submits to

Weightlessness, I welcome my spirit to transcend

White sound with silence and beckon the peace

Wrap me like velvet, the hold grazes the skin

To remind me when comfort remained

And wasn't drained by the Ideals of never...

I love space, because I get to imagine a world

Less close to real, I get to drift into a feeling

That keeps highs and lows at bay

With the posture of surety that

Fades in the milk of unhinged

Truths and tarnished Skies and hearts

That never breathed, I feel like A cosmic

Can some cleanse the current space of being

In a dream less imagined and transform all outcries

To reality. What are the rest of the sounds like?

What are the rest of the planets like

Could we speak to not?

Could we seek to dream and never stop?

And silence the noise Of never?

I wonder?

Welcome more of the night to kiss the ground

And the brown cheeks of a lost girl.

Revive Me

Smokey trails in the rare view

Rolling mountains overlooking

City highs and stifled air waves

REVIVAL

That widen ways of on coming

Mobile streams we jam up like

Bulky cars and choppy concrete

On heated streets keeping the rhythm

On soft tips and wet lips to speak

Life in wind stream, draw closer like

The inhale of a Mary Jane we high off

The chemistry that lays between the

Raised passions of deep kisses and long

Gazes that crack the soul's code of the endow

Pouring stocks of emotions the size of

Body bags if we got the clout to take a bet

On our hearts path will you unlock-

The Hidden spaces beneath the surface,

Of groove and a love trance?

I coupled the 44 with the 26

And still came up with an 8

wrapping 6 on an entrance

Inhaling the fumes you spew that keep me

Wasted with coherent words to unpack into

The confines of your dresser draws to dress

You in every piece the blended fibers

Of my love capsule, let me rain on

you like the tropics high precipitation

A boundless rain season wet with
Tears and sweat that keeps
The adrenaline rushing in heated intimacy,
We walk knocking skin biting
And sucking ourselves into another
Dimension where our existence flies high
Resisting the ups and downs holding hands
Promising to never let go. My thoughts swell up
When left solo. I'm day dreaming till the
Time when my head meets your chest again,
Where we interlock bodies, laced fingers
Legs intertwined, where we gaze deep to
Speak to each other "you're mine" the thing
About a deep soul bond is we soar amidst the
Greatest company and dwell in the lengthy
Waves of our own frequency, our only destiny
Is to match the last moments we stole
When kissing under moonlight and twinkling
Starlights in a rich midnight sky we get wavy
In secret talks and long walks, rendezvous and
Trouble tones and base that cancels the treble
And leave the melody of the synchrony of
Our chocolate waves in a sea of depth sinking
Like quicksand when our hands clutch I feel

REVIVAL

Your pulse like a vibration to a new lifeline

Letting go is not an option

We rise and fall fuss and fight,

kiss and hug, keep up to make love and find lines

in between words unspoken yet felt

It's like having your heart renewed

When your soulmates are talking.

Solo nights welcome lonely,

Yet thinking of you brings me comfort

Like every thing felt is a blanket to hold

My body close

We rise and fall kiss blindly

Knowing the light is hovering

for a slow drain off our unmatched ecstasy.

We rhyme and laugh, plan and drive

We celebrate in all the ways,

keeping the sense in tight fists

Realizing there is no one like, but,

Just you and I we unravel in the safety net of our being,

exposing the truths that make us naked you

make my walls fall and your voice is like a soothing

lullaby to all of me that is unknown.

I want a ticket to the escape, that is you.

Pumped with a certain kind of fear something

Tells me our beginning is near and you have my

Back no matter the match. Solo nights renamed

That area that you market in warm sheets

That left your scent behind.

Your memory is easy to revisit and travel

So effortlessly your heart is giving

And so is your time

I keep thinking a lucky one I am

To share the words

"you're mine"

Solo nights keep my mind wondering,

you became my best friend when the lights went dim

you kept the flame flickering matching mine.

Until our next sessions which welcome

long lasting discussions in a mind.

Creative Well

Ears are like funnels to the esophagus

pumping truth on vibrating lyrics

traveling my contemplations

through my fingertips,

dancing ever so pleasantly

Like drifting keys on piano...

it can be that sweet .

or rough, like sand storms in the Sahara desert,

Prickling your pores just as a reflex

to check if you're listening.

I was once asked how do I define artistry,

back tracking towards age seven where

I found a free flow to the unknown.

Scripted manuscripts for deaf tones

and wasn't far from the most high

I plaster praises on blank pages hoping

my ink can somehow write me a salvation.

When asked, what is artistry?..

I left the question between a margin and blank space

between blue lines that reflect

The colors of veins and said...

Listen, I generated conversation on stages from

spoken words to scripted plays

fostering a continuation in sequels for

screen hoping that your experience

is depicted for the masses, to turn the unheard

into a brand new radio,

When I speak it's Yetunde,

the ancestors didn't feel that all their

prayers were answered so God created me,

when I speak mesh your senses to

the white noise and tap your heart as it rocks rhythm,

cause the Lords speaking,

Leaking, flowing freely using me

As the last hope and vessel...

To teach and maybe resurrect a dead feeling

Knowledge and anecdotes unsung

I'm the connecting junction

between the dead and the living,

often times we mope aimlessly

Never realizing that we lost...

meaningful, that's why it's so easy

for brothers to kill without reason

because pain became so numb that

they curl pointers on triggers...

neglect, trespassed the development

of anything pleasantly momentous where pain,

replaced love, cause nowadays it's just easier,

Posting blame on broken edifices

that most recall as home,

But home don't sound familiar,

It's much like the back lashes

from masters whips that out line our

cultures, tailor made to our genetic makeup

and it's no surprise that laughter stunts our growth,

corners harbor all secret windows,

somehow it's safer than solitude with self

I'm a blacksmith to past and future, unlocking

things concealed and daring to call it a discovery,

I do it without question

Even when repercussions are so painful

To the point of self mutilation, gouging dreams

and passion from belly for lost mothers and girls

Whom seemed to still be fetuses

Because no one paid attention

where, cycles run repeatedly like chains to pedals,

and peddling is survival

I castrate my soul as a sacrifice

when entering the realm of performance

This word baptized me and

I use it as my first and last resort

To safety.

I need no weapons of mass destruction

just give me a bag,

Of paper, pens, a dictionary and all the

experiences that corrosively

wrap around the spinal cords of humanity,

ingredients to always be creative,

Provide an open mic and an open stage so me

and the rest of the ministry can Rip it

We spit till our skin turns red to blackness,

onyx pure and out of it came obsidian

Queen Goddess to God I am Given hence Naima,

you have just been cordially invited

To my cerebral theater, placing beats on junction,

fusing my funky coiled soul on

forging positions, tired of being pregnant

so they force there way out, dare not

be a vision of pursuit but a complex dissertation

of a swollen stratosphere

barring all these souls waiting to be

freed using me to offer it vocally,

Employed by the dynamic devise

often mentioned as art,

but I insist you redirect your thinking…

This is a way of life, when your core

is not reached unless put your heart on it

passion drives you so in other words you'll die for it,

do everything with a whole heart,

no barter to carter or indecent

Exchanges for a temporary fix

I am a fortress to the conjunction of the hub

better known as the artistic circular

My two feet plant sections...

On complicated implications

Joining hands with solidarity

Of personal individualistic expression

Question: Tell me how hot the sun is?

Because Fire and Water defines my anatomy

How quick can we start an eruption??

Letter Stanza

Your, intentions are not what brew from your soul,

you're counter acting your,

Qualities with substitution,

supplementary additives hoping to eventually

Yank realness out of the bellies

Of counterfeit chemistries,

Your experiments are not successful,

You're lacking patience...

Expecting infinite locations.

Silencing your voice on the strength

Of "what if." Instead of "Why not."

I mean, you're beautiful.

Woman so pure and your walk commands to

Demand the attention you're seeking,

and draws in the ones most

Detrimental to the development of your spirit.

Wise women stepped before you,

Losing site of where you've been

Is the most disappointing thing you could ever do.

The pain endured is hard to combat alone,

Miraculously overcoming hurdles

Like an Olympic track star

No one has ever seen you break down

Nervously and cry...

Thinking your spirit is too open to be human

Therefore walls are much better.

The truth is, not being able to really

bask in the ambiance of touch ,

Makes you act reckless,

best decisions become failed possibilities

You go to war, when ever vulnerability

knocks at the door, because

Intruders left, eyeballs and hearts on the floor

and they all look, like yours

Developing more dead memories

than genocides in foreign countries

You separate occupation and

Matriculation in institutions,

like secretary and state.
In all actuality they are one in the same.

Your speech is eloquently seasoned and nothing short of
Passion...
Lady you're woman, Nubian goddess,
soft to touch like ancestors dipped in tar,
What I'm saying is, you're obsidian, your diligence is impeccable.
Masking your beauty with tough qualities,
figuring edgy, is more acceptable, than feminine.
Men don't cherish that.
Since they are most familiar to harder
and often erect, you think, maybe, it's better this way.
Mind, body and soul are often unattended
when dismissive, devious tactics are induced
to lay with you indecently.
Finding boxes for your sex like a caricature.
While you're screaming "I'm human."
Or maybe they'll lay promissory notes
on your emotions while laying naked
yet clothed enough to remain whole;
then swiftly tell you, they have to go.
Or maybe, they'll keep you at arms length,
just so you don't get a way, but have no

Intentions of crowning you Queen…

Mean while you question,

If love is even for you.

Blacking your heart with

The pain spoon fed as gourmet meals.

Forgetting the beauty surrounding you.

Friends who are kin to you.

Family that will uplift,

Surround build and destroy in order

For your existence to subsist.

Beauty in all dimensions, instead your suppress,

settle and collect payments on walking flesh

between your thighs and in nonchalant kisses.

While daydreaming of the man,

Your heart most desires

though you have never met.

You know his walk, talk,

Creative being and intellect,

As if you birthed him from

The lining of the bleeding midnight sky,

Your loneliness swallows trunks of sadness,

Laying blindly to define the line of preciousness

to far to taste, now it's burned

Into chunks of a painful memory.

You need to be revived, vital and ready,
recalling everything you've known
And open to the unknown,
He's gentle like the green-blue sea,
His mind's eye is carefully placed
in the locator of righteousness
He's most tentative to love and others.
Gorgeously human, charming and handsome,
Respects the spirit and follows
The rhythm of his heart.
Yet you'll ruin all prospective
Chances if your vision is blurred,
Indolent to your spirit! Not acceptable
You're Naima Yetunde,
You possess the strength of the women
Of your ancestors and family.
Those around you depend on that.
Your wisdom
Tenaciousness,
fiery personality
and energy are
Are transcended from various elements

and channeling

Through you.

A strong king will depend on you too.

Two sides to a street, with one way to go.

Live fully or not at all. Fear not. Dream forever.

Liberation

Let me start by saying Perfection

isn't ordained by any human,

Nor does it lay in the palms of my touch

I've endured mistakes and mutual

Pain but my intentions

Remained while, always true,

Never in vain or

Chocolate covered for sweet notions

And sugared franks for virgin ears

But Immersed into the ideal volcano of poison

I traced my fears on the lining of your skin

And watched you hold my tears in your pores

As if to bare my luggage from the stress on my back

Like your honesty was more pure

Than your devious actions,

Like, broken eagle wings in the blanket of the sky

REVIVAL

I made love with convictions and conversations

And fed our souls with laughter

I struggled with the rope while tossing my own

Morals under the integrity

Brewed from my entity

Forgetting my beauty in the

Pupils of your windows understanding now

That I was never nor will I ever be

Of importance, I treated me

Second to your acceptance

put right over left as I rumbled

With the bones of dead love

Never to be removed from 6ft

Like drowning houses in Katrina

I flooded like its sister to a tsunami,

Now at the forefront of a

Torn womb and broken love letters

That shred like a house with termites,

I still found happiness under the rocks of jurisdiction

While conversing with God I asked for a word

Of deliverance and maybe this

Is my redemption, salvation let this paper soak

My reason to back track,

Rewind and revisit the site of, "what if,"

Tired of being second to best

Down right...Not good enough...

Buried in glistening sunset

Horizons that seduces my flesh

Pulling reasoning to the back burner

And burn rubber under my feet

Temporary satisfaction form

Wounds on organs breathing inward then out

Backtrack like train tracks malfunctioned

And I'm my own train wreck

But in this I redeem all beauty

I am without your approval

Finding peace at the core

Of all things of my being

Independent and rebuking abandonment

From my existence so today and beyond

I thank you and love you, I'll blink twice

And hopefully hold hands with one who

Will treat me like the universe on a quest for Freedom.

Chapter Six
A DEDICATION FOR THE COOL

A Tribute To Mommy

Hey Momma! You are smooth like

A jazz blues melody

Your tones and tunes match the

Beauty in your hues

You're liquorish and bible gum

You're collard greens and

Black eyed peas

You're special in the sense

Of a treat to the world you deem yours

You're number one first and remaining

Queen. Your energy is varied

In all the ways you express,

you have that knowledge

And text stands no test.

Look over there!

A horizon big as the eye can see,

Looking closer I see in the distance

A woman you conquers the waves

And the sea. Her humor ricochets

Off the drums in the distance.

Making laughter a noise maker

Her creative nature flows

Oh so effortlessly. She's got

Pockets of designs hinged

At her finger tips

I mean after all she created me

Her offspring as a testate to greatness

We honor you as our carrier to live

Boundlessly. Her hugs envelope

The depths of our souls like an endless

Black hole, her smile reminds us

Of the direction of the light

Her journey gives hope that we

Have all the might.

Here intellect is impressive grand by

The worlds delight, her patience is

Grand for those that are more near than far

A DEDICATION FOR THE COOL

Her heart is soft and wide

Because of her we are all stars.

My mommy, thinking of you

Brings smiles and joy

Followed by deep appreciation

For all that you are!

You're sugar and spice and everything nice

You're sweet and polite and such a delight

Your presence is bit in the eyes that you hold dear

You're close like the melanin in yo' skin.

You keep us grounded in the belief in the

Highest God. Your love is large,

wide and unmatched by any

Your special and pure like a pot full of honey

YOU ARE Momma, mommy, woman, Queen

Warrior, survivor, lover of words and art

Black and white films, music, dance

And you inspire us all

Your patience is awesome in every sense of the word

God knew what he was doing when he made us a pair

There are not enough words to really express

How thankful, I truly am. Cherish these tokens

Now and forever more

A tribute of many that rest at my core

Wishing you an abundance of joy and

Living your best life!

More triumphs to overcome

And you do so with so much grace

You juggle those hats, without

tilting your crown. I am simply humbled

To have been blessed to call you momma.

My mommy, my Shero, the woman I'll forever honor

When the Star met the Sun And realized he was a star too!

When a brown skin girl

With a bright smile and a broken *Skip it*

Looked into the eyes of a

Man who would soon,

Mean more to her than words could compose.

Instantly, resembling everything

Transparently, genuine,

He Poured power into her soul with "hello,

What's your name?"

Eager and extremely vocal

Young with pigtails

And sun kissed skin,

She looked up and replied

"Naima"

A DEDICATION FOR THE COOL

Often I reflect on the times

We shared to comfort or

Calm my raging soul.

Feeling like Men Always Leave And you,

Seemed to not only stay,

But came as an Angel for my mom

Myself and later Kedar.

You are full of funny jokes

And surity that would

Follow the phrase...

"I Bet You A Fat Man on a Stick"

Forgettable and reminders

And yet you never forgot the little girl you first

Laid eyes on at the tender age of nine

And instantly deemed me your star.

To be a guiding light for a man

To see the beauty in me, to want to be a

Driving force to protect, love and continue

To support at all cost and blood ain't sign

My name to yours

I say...thank God for all that he is.

You have a way with words

That are creative, rooted in your accent

and the depth of your proud

Acknowledgement of

"I am from West Palm Beach Florida...

Growing up they called me, Bay boy."

Though your path has been nothing short

Of tdramateous I find it

So incredible fragile in the

Ideal space of special that love

Extended and overflowed on my mom and without

hesitation , you made me your own too

At nine years old, I felt the magnitude

of this like the

Drawing of horseshoe magnets

affixed to the bottom of your shoes,

so that anywhere you stepped with us,

it was forever planted.

Forever love grew and grew

and when I doubted any love a man can give,

I have always said, thank God for

The man who showed up and out

So that I would know and never forget

Who I am and how special I am to just him.

A space that cannot be replaced.

From scrapped, elbows, knees and keloids,

Playdates with friends that
Always turned into the best cooking
Experience of our lives,
Because it always involved Pizza or candy.

Your unique laugh, your willingness
to be so available for all that I ever need.
For the many years of advice,
for being there for all my many track meets,
poetry engagements,
performances,
Graduations
and so much more,
for my first date at 16 years old
to demonstrate the standards
for which I should accept.
At times I might have fallen short
of maintaining the standard you
worked so hard to exemplify...
A time or two you came to me saying
"Babe I gave you the game in your hand"
But you never judged me
you never made me feel any less
loved or special.

For me, just for me...

I realized you are a man who is my father,

That will forever and always

Stay and come back for me.

I love you beyond words.

Happy Fathers Day.

Naima-Your Star

When Little Fire Met the Rock

The man who said, "I will always know you"

A tender girl like me, valued the shoes

You filled, while planting glimmers of light

In the innocent lives of youth like mine.

I called to you for guidance with a wild

Pen a paper that became a leading kite

My only dad was my step-father and

You like an irreplaceable uncle,

that reminded me of the direction of my star.

An abandoned child stumbled upon

Two angels in men, my step-father Leon

And Mr.B-

Who demonstrated that real men never leave.

A DEDICATION FOR THE COOL

We started off as mentor to mentee

And later blossomed to family, not needing

Any ounce of blood to define us.

We were late to open mics and meetings at Petey's.

School yards and round table workshops-

That circled us like city street blocks

We were Central Park and Harlem.

Little Fire and Rock man, we were soul

Of Brooklyn and Jollof Beats.

We were corner stores and hip hop

Stretches between Brooklyn and Queens-

Manhattan, Westchester and everything in between.

There will never be enough

Words for what you mean to me

Accept this low level token

As a tribute too for true

A King and parent to even a little girl like me.

Writing you this tribute is delayed and overdue

Please excuse my delay as life

Has a way of butting in.

Tears swell my eyes and blinks

Melt them in my skin

All happy tears you see

That God blessed me with a teacher

Friend like you, who is so dear to me.

I often think of where—

I would be had you not asked

"Do you write?"

The thought of not realizing my

Full voice in poetry and all the magic

I hone with words

Sometimes all it takes-

To be at the right place

At the right time

To transform someone's life,

For this lifetime

I am so overjoyed that someone was mine.

I always say you have many kids in these streets.

16 years later

"I'll always know you,"

Is still with me—

I hope this birthday present isn't too late,

In fact my prayer is that it reaches you far past any hatch.

Celebrating Your 90 Years

90 years of Grace

The most beautiful way

This word holds Power

Coupled with dignified

The four words combined,

Powerful, graceful, dignified woman

Is the best way to identify-

The matriarch of Our family. Rubie

Parker. Rubie with an I.E "not" to be

mistaken for y There is no "why" to be

described

Your greatness,

Your value to-this realm of life.

You have blessed many,

Loved by all, humbled by your journey.

I am honored to be amongst your blood

We all gather here, on this day to celebrate

Your life, and honor your name,

You are surrounded by the power

Your grace introduced to the very fabric

Of spanning generations, we call you

momma, sister, auntie, friend, wife and-

many other hats you wear to match-

your reflective choice of style

You stand tall in all.

Your beauty is elegance

Your presentation to the world-

Is nothing less than dynamic, super fly

And in today's words the young folks would say—

you my dear have swagger.

Reflections of your power,

Can be found in the success of your children

The brightness in the eyes and

Smiles of your grandchildren.

Because of you I am Yetunde

Sharing a birthday with your

Wonderful mother Irene Elvira Thornhill Jordan

By my name, I am reminded—

Of the special link in the bloodline.

The tokens of knowledge you bestowed

Beneath the memories,

You captured in photographs

Cards preserved; travels around the world.

Your resilience is remarkable

A young woman clever

Spicy with a sense of serious humor.

Always ready to break into a song

Or show off your moves on the dance floor,

A DEDICATION FOR THE COOL

The beats, carry your vehicle to express.

Voyaged to the United States

At 18 years of age from Panama

Desiring to make this place home.

You became home to many family members,

Who journeyed far,

With the same fire in their

Hearts and eyes for better.

We remember.

Your Spiciness, spunky and loving heart

Lead you to a love in Theodore Parker

Coupled, your love, joyful, fun, humorous ways—

Were infectious

We remember

Your commitment to your community

Love for church and God,

And your generosity is admirable

We embrace you,

We cherish you and

We will always remember

Cheers to Auntie Rubie Parker,

That's Rubie with an I.E not to be

Mistaken for "Y" there is no "why"

To be described you are

And always will be valued,

Cherished and loved.

For your spiciness, for your generosity

For your love, for your dedication.

There is no better way to

Describe the matriarch

Of our family, other than---

A graceful, powerful and dignified woman

Today we celebrate you and your 90 years of grace.

Happy Birthday!

Love Always

Naima Yetunde Ince

4/18/2017

For You My Love

Time has traveled around

Us until the moment in time,

Our respective passion for

The entertainment industry

Sparked conversations that

Seemed to be endless.

There has always been a particular connection,

One that desired attention that

I felt I could not entertain and give,

Provided the circumstances.

Life and God have an

Interesting way of showing you

Differently So much that it is undeniably so.

My admiration and respect

for you grows Everyday and

I always say I am blessed to have a friend

And so much more in you.

Our journey to falling in love seemed

Sudden, when in fact it was always there.

Two staring, piercing through

Our soul windows to acknowledge

That we were more than just friends

More than just partners we realized

We're twin flames.

When I felt broken and not valuable

You reminded me just how special I am
You made it your mission to demonstrate
That to me, everyday and in every way.

You held my hand through
Some of the most trying times.
You supported me and stood by me
When others seem to fade into the distance.

Your love is ever present
Ever real and ever giving.
Thank you for not just accepting me
Into your life as your friend
Business partner
Then woman.
Thank you for accepting
My most precious, baby boy
Who has my entire heart,
Now you both have that in common.

For being a shoulder, loving
And a friend to him.
For listening to his many
Questions and lending to his inquisitive mind

For encouraging him and sharing

A piece of you and love, endlessly.

For making him feel that you are

Dependable and being a leading

Example on how you love me and

Made sure to shower him with the same.

The ups and downs

The conflicts, the resolutions,

The many fun times we share,

The laughs and most of all the dreams,

I know all of that is possible if we stay

Faithful and true.

I do not want to do life without you.

Lenox and I are so very blessed

And thankful to have you.

Thank you for being a friend,

A father figure to Lenox and then so much more.

I know this is one

Of many Father's Days we will share together.

Enjoy your day love,

You deserve it!

Naima-Boobie/Grandma

NYI&Q

The Greatest Boy

My loving son
Who stole his momma's heart
The ones whose eyes lights up the sky
The one whose skin is nice and brown
The one who knows to protect his crown
The one whose spirit is wild and profound
The one whose willful and kind
The one who knows to keep others in mind
The one who taught me patience and love
The one who reminds me to go the distance
To fulfill every dream I extend the same to you
Remember no one can take your freedom from you
It's as bright and wild as you want it to be
Deep inside your soul extending through your heart
Keep God in all things and you will be blessed
Remember to acknowledge your carriers
Fight for what's right and never sway

Live to the full extent of happy
Dare to take risks that others shy from

Build your network and earn your net worth

Develop a family in love of God and family

Remember the soul of your momma

Keep the fire large and wide

Remember your brown skin is your power

Not your failure no matter the images you see

Or lies you hear, keep true to yourself and others

Embrace your blackness and pass that power

Onto your wife and children

You are my greatest gift

You have my blood in ya

You have power and love

You have gumption and dreams

You have liveliness and beauty

You have the drive and will to

Fight and live your best life

Don't let them take your mind

For you are as special as a rare

Diamond and so much more

You are the largest gem that

Anyone would have the pleasure of meeting

Your quick and witty, smart and creative

Intelligent and worthy you

Are everything that a King should and will be

You are the light of my life

The extra beat in my heart

The reason I breathe

And so very much more

You could never know

How deep my love goes

Just know that it forever flows

This dedication is to the part

Of me that will never die

Take me with you in all that

You do and see how far you can fly

I love you dearly now and forever

Remember this piece when the chips

Fall wacky and you feel like you just can't go on

You have strength and will to get through anything

You were built for this for you are

A black boy who will become a black man and you

Are always and always will be King

Love always and forever

Your momma

Let me start by saying Perfection

isn't ordained by any human,

Nor does it lay in the palms of my touch

I've endured mistakes

And mutual pain but my intentions

Remained while, always true, never in vain or

Chocolate covered for sweet notions

And sugared franks for virgin ears

But Immersed into the ideal volcano of poison

I traced my fears on the lining of your skin

And watched you hold my tears in your pores

As if to bare my luggage from the stress on my back

Like your honesty was more pure

Than your devious actions,

Like, broken eagle wings in the blanket of the sky,

I made love with convictions and conversations

And fed our souls with laughter,

I struggled with the rope while tossing my own

Morals under the integrity

brewed from my entity

Forgetting my beauty in the

Pupils of your windows understanding now

That I was never nor will I ever be

Of importance, I treated me

Second to your acceptance

put right over left as I rumbled

With the bones of dead love

Never to be removed from 6ft

Like drowning houses in Katrina

I flooded like its sister to a tsunami,

Now at the forefront of a torn

Womb and broken love letters

That shred like a house with termites,

I still found happiness under the rocks of jurisdiction

While conversing with God I asked for a word

Of deliverance and maybe this

Is my redemption, salvation let this paper soak

My reason to back track,

Rewind and revisit the site of, "what if,"

Tired of being second to best

Down right, not good enough,

Buried in glistening sunset horizons

That seduces my flesh

Pulling reasoning to the back burner

And burn rubber under my feet,

Temporary satisfaction form

Wounds on organs breathing inward then out,

Backtrack like train tracks malfunctioned

And I'm my own train wreck

But in this I redeem all beauty

I am without your approval

Finding peace at the core of all things of my being

Independent and rebuking abandonment

From my existence so today and beyond

I thank you and love you, I'll blink twice

And hopefully hold hands with one who

Will treat me like the universe on a quest for Freedom.

A Dedication To Her

If I could go back and warn you

20 times I would, if I could

Go back and warn you about the fires

The danger and everything in between I would

But what go will that do like is about learning

So that you can overcome and have a testimony to share

I wanted to dedicate this poem to you

Say take care of yourself even more

Remember to always stay true to yourself and your values

Don't apologize for being bold and taking risks

For they take you far and when the sun seems

Dull you keep following the light

Eventually it will get bright

Be Careful of who you give your all to

Not everyone will give their all to you

Listen to your intuition for it always knows

And don't second guess which way that it goes

I wanted to dedicate this poem to you

To let you know just how much I love you

Your drive and passion is oh so sexy

Your love and compassion is far and wide

Your intelligence and talent is out of this world

You give it all a shot at 100 percent and let nothing

Or no one stand in your way

When the chips fell and you lost your way

You looked for a new route and eventually

Found the way, when you got tired

And had no idea what you were going to do

You fell down on your knees hugged yourself

And prayed for better days

And a word to show you the way

All these things make you persistent

But triumphant

In your own unique way

And I have to tell you

I am so glad you saw your way

Through to brighter days

If I had to give you any advice it would be

Never stop being you because

You are simply amazing

I know one thing that is very true, you believe

You pray you hold on for dear life

Till you see yourself through

I wrote this dedication just for her Naima Yetunde the Queen you are

Chapter Seven
BROWN SKIN POWER

Love Is

Love is God

Love is justice

Love is ever flowing

Love is knowing

Love is welcoming

Love is unconditional

Love is a principle

Love is profoundly special

Love is Powerful and crucial

Love is gentle

Love is plentiful

Love is kind

Love is mine

My love is too overflowing

To have thrown away

My love is too compassionate to

Have thrown away

My love is too true

To have thrown away

My love is too forever to

Have thrown away

My love is to always to have

Thrown away

My love is too

Cool to have

Thrown away

Love is calling

Hearts to travel

Keeping kindness

In the front seat

Lets love more

And angle this

Towards the love

You deem is too

Loyal to have thrown away

You Can't Say Shit

This has been on my mind

It's always there like the

Melanin in my skin

Try living your life

With a bullseye on your back

Concerned about how

You will live from day to day

Just because your skin is brown

Or black the many hues we are

As brown skin people

There is power in who we are

And everything that makes us glow

We are the very essence of everything Magical

Truth is walking down the street

Running, riding a bike, driving a car

Playing in playgrounds

Out on a porch or stoop

That could be the very last thing you do

before Becoming a hashtag

Don't dare to empathize with

Us you have no idea what it's like

Waiting by doors hoping your husband

Son, brother, cousin returns home on time

Knowing that we made it another day

Without getting gunned down

Let's get real-till you

Have to teach your

5 year old son how to operate

If a car he is in ever gets pulled over

How to play in the playground without

Looking like a threat, how to speak to

White people just so they won't say he is

Being disrespectful and suddenly go

From the name you gave them to "boy"

You have no idea what it feels like

To look on to the news reports

And see so many faces that look like

Yours dead unjustly over and over

And over and over and over and over

Over and over, over, over again

How many times our men

Are killed or thrown in jail

unjustly, taken from their families

Their children unnecessarily

You have no idea
What that pain feels like
Don't get upset
When these conversations
Are always on the tips of
Our tongues
Share images of those
We lost
Protest and riot
Just to try to defend our bodies
And say we deserve to live
Fighting to prove why our life matters
Just like yours

Don't you dare tell us how to act
Because there is no other way
To fight

My son is a brown skin boy
Who will grow into a man
And the fear the surrounds my heart
You could never understand or even imagine

. . .

So yeah you don't know what this feels like

Stop acting like you are equivalent

Saying you're tired of hearing this

Over and over again.

We're tired of being killed

Just for existing over and over again

This country was built on our backs

This country was built around fear of us

Because of the color of our skin

And the talents, our intelligence

We have been objectified and not

Valued as human beings.

So yeah don't get mad

When we turn up and

Get loud and make noise

As far and wide as we can

Just trying to survive

We are out here surviving

More than we are living

My tears stream

Alongside the mothers

Who cry out for their babies

Slaughtered on camera

My tears stream down

For the children who

Never see daylight

Past the age of 15

Because you thought

Their life was not worthy

My tears and my heart aches

Because yes I know them

They are my

Brothers

Sisters

Mother

Father

Aunts

Uncles

Cousins

Friends

They are one of US

Period.

Black Queen

Girl you are beautiful

The tones in your skin

Illuminate with the sun

Your features are exotic

And profound

Your mind is powerful

And worth all the pennies

For the thoughts you harbor

Your heart is pure

Like gold

You traveled here

Unknowingly

Shackled and bounded

You came with culture

And real soil beneath your feet

You didn't ask to be here

You were enslaved and transformed

Forced into a system that degraded

Everything you are and everything your stand for

Humiliated you and your family

Stripped of everything beautiful and begged to

Be anything more than an object

They secretly lusted after you

They took your gems and pocketed them for sale

They undid your worth, time and time again

Fast forward to the present

Everyone wants to model you

Wear your skin

Build your hips

Curves and lips

Yet no one wants to let you in the room

Sit at those executive tables

Just because even still

Your curly hair

And dark skin

All are still the wrong types for entry

I'll tell you this your roots are so deep

They run miles around the world

Between oceans

Your intelligence is needed

You build nations and empires

Conquer obstacles and rule the world

Your brown skin is smooth

And beautiful just like pearls

All of this makes you bold and powerful

This they cannot take away from you

You are queen

You are mother

You are doctor

You are lawyer

You are dreamer

You are business owner

You are creator in all sense of the word

You are great and nothing or no

One can measure up to you

Beautiful you are

Black King

You are mighty

You are powerful

And so special to us

They objectified you

Degraded you in front of your women

Discarded you and made you

Nothing but a "thing"

It's so important that

You understand

How much we need you

How much we treasure you

And how beautiful you are

Your skin tells stories

The scars worth

Soothing your roots

Are so deep they travel

Miles around this world

And deep and wide across the seas

The oceans and everything in between

The waves crash to the sound

Of your heartbeat

Your leadership is needed

Your intelligence is necessary

To redefine the future

Empowering you is our

duty, uplifting you should

Be a part of our daily routine

Let us lift you up when the world rejects you

When they notice nothing

But the color of your skin

Your features are unique

Embrace your curly hair

And full lips

Endowment and all that makes you man

You are our protectors

Your are our fathers

Community leaders

We cannot live without you

For you are mighty

Enlarged Vision

Looking through the lens with full eyes

Soaking in the sights with full eyes

Detecting details, down to the

Smallest, soaking in the sights

The ones, I cannot unseen

Fixed in a memory

Remind me of the flavors

In my skin.

One that holds the stench

Of bodies smothered in tight quarters

Reminding me what a fight feels like

Reminding me of the power,

That wears me like the melanin

In my skin.

The kind that reflects

The God deep within

From the day I was created

Yes...Looking through that Lens.

What's Your Position-Remix

My Brother is a Nigger

My sister is a Nigger

And, well, I'm a Nigger too,

That's what my master said right

We walk these streets

Seeds reaped in scorned nourishment

Names disrespected, changing ourselves

Because of what they say

Forgetting our history attached the chains,

Linked to epilogues never printed like Motto

So they never taught us shit, we had first hand

Degradation, hands on experience to the real definition

Of black-- incompetent, ugly, uneducated, animalistic, coon, Porch Monkey

Our unique exotic beauty summed

It into one word -- unacceptable,

Stripped of all identity, adding Nigger to the roster

We sell ourselves out before sticking together

Desensitize our archaic wisdom

Factoring in our own pathetic

Rationalized thinking

To why we are still niggers,

N.I.G.G.A.S or Z drop the ER

Cause that's disrespect homie.

2007 Jena 6 committed a crime

Defending their integrity, threatened

For their lives. Nooses posted on tree branches

Awaiting their throats paying homage to the old ways

Twisted inhumane brains call it a horrific school Prank.

I wonder if Megan was laughing.

Bet you pain didn't tickle.

Propane in her insides was never-ending torture.

Her soul's fiery spirit, drained of scarlet wine

As her captors toasted her torment.

And still...

You continue to use the word Nigga

My lyrics paint onyx truths on the headstones never

Marked. Derived from ancestors

in the core of suffocated silhouettes

Gargled blood and invaded

wombs mixed spiritual hymn songs

The word doesn't change

meaning based on the spelling

Usage just confines souls to mental slavery

Constantly digging a whole in

Unmarked grave plots

Next to one of your ancestors

That righteously died by it

Against it, for it just so

you could be called your name.

My Last Breath

In my last breath I choke the syllables

of freedom chasing the adrenalin

in my veins flowing to my

heartbeat gripping tight to survival in the

crustacean of all my fears

I rock planets with the mic tight in base

beats like base heads knocking to their last hit.

I flex notations on canvas blocks, pinpointing

my last step in the last breath, inhale

slow while executing the soft sounds

of baby breath on the rhyme

messaged into my skin, above the rim

floating high overseas flights

while pulsating lyric and gyrating bodies,

watch this flow tight in

endless ultrasound, they try to mussel my

deliverance and snap

shackles around perfected purpose

frequencies with propaganda in the

passenger seat,

I'm their biggest paranoia
Like the thought of change
Globally, seeping in like CNN
Broadcasting tragedies
behind broadcast prophecies in my last breath
I tell those I love them when they fear it,
Blanket my thoughts on lined paper and
margin the real in chosen
Vessels, hug the world with
The deepest story tales from the depth of
My diaphragm, clench my womb,
eternal pregnancy of ultra light
Reflecting the glow of chocolate

sun in the star light, tomorrow isn't

Promised so I build hope in destitution,

it's my order in human court,

Cause daddy never saw it and moms hugs

were those wrapped around

Survival amethyst rocks, morphed into lighting

through my palms,

Call me a Dragon Ball Z character

Phenomenon unstitched but etched into the

Fabric of beauty, Goddess, obsidian, queen, voice

--- untamed, dreams-----

Unleashed so I pull

Smooth like the herb in your L

that makes you gaze into

Starlit skies pumping your

heartbeat into drum machines,

Unstoppable, quick with it, slow with it.

Pull quicker in my last breath

I'll heal the world with these

Manuscripts of stories

Unchosen, unborn fetuses that

withdrew in the limelight so they

Labeled me their Barrier,

in tuned short stopper,

with a dream in the belt strapped across my

permeated lungs manifesting reality,

Gasping quicker, trying to encapsulate all

the visions escaped, tucked under

The tongues of the dead,

I got 2 milliseconds to make the earth shake,

I'm an earthquake from Cali-forn-ia

on your mental safe, sea shells

Knock ocean sounds to eardrums crashing

The pronunciation of my name,

Since water is relentless and unable

To capture through fingertips

To the spread of tangible flesh, so is my last breath.

Chapter Eight
BONUS

Baby I often

Question how we got here

Mainly because is so

Beautifully unexpected

In the way in which it

Sought my heart

There's no question it's destined

Time with you is intense

Powerfully compact

Instantly catered to a space

Of forever yearning

Till never ending

Forevers that wrap tight like cuffs

I'm yearning for you now

And even after

I love the way we sink and seep

Into each other endlessly our chemistry

Travels like light bolts

Through us our touch is electrifying

In between swallow the beats

That still the spaces in a dream

Where we design the outcome

I'll follow you, I'll dream and create

Design space with only you

That we inhabit I am yearning for the depth

In your soul please touch mine endlessly,

Endlessly until the end of time

My heart, soul, mind, body and spirit

Are in agreement that you are

Certainly mine, cause

Baby often I...

www.ingramcontent.com/pod-product-compliance
Lightning Source LLC
Chambersburg PA
CBHW071404290426
44108CB00014B/1682